Planet Protectors

CREATURE KEEPER

BookLife PUBLISHING

A catalogue record for this book is available from the British Library.

ISBN: 978-1-78637-652-7

Written by:
John Wood

Edited by:
Kirsty Holmes

Designed by:
Drue Rintoul

PHOTO CREDITS

All images are courtesy of Shutterstock.com. With thanks to Getty Images, Thinkstock Photo and iStockphoto. Front Cover – R-studio, plavevski. Throughout – Nadzin. 2 – JWPhotoworks. 4&5 – Vectorpocket, Stock_VectorSale. 6&7 – Tom Grundy, Rich Carey. 8&9 – Oceloti, brown32. 10&11 – Rudmer Zwerver, FloridaStock. 12&13 – natrot, Titov Nikolai. 14&15 – Rich Carey, pokku. 16&17 – MaxyM, algae, vladwel, Tigergallery. 18&19 – TFoxFoto, Birkir Asgeirsson. 20&21 – robuart, monkeyjump. 22&23 – mything, Netta07, Jabirki Art, Michael Moloney.

CONTENTS

Words that look like **this** can be found in the glossary on page 24.

Time for a Mission

There are four Planet Protectors. We've looked after the **environment** since the beginning of time.

The world is not looking healthy. We need somebody to join our team and help us save it. Could that be you? Come along. We're going on a mission.

There will be questions throughout this book. Write down your answer to each one and check your score at the end!

Our base is called Trashy Island. It is a fortress made out of recycled stuff.

A Load of Rubbish

Rubbish can be harmful to many animals.

If only people would recycle their plastic items... Then the plastic could be used again and again, instead of ending up in a **landfill site** – or worse!

When plastic bags are thrown away, they can end up in the ocean. Turtles might accidentally eat them. This is dangerous!

There is a mountain of rubbish blocking our path! There is no way around. It looks like this is your first test!
At the end, your answers can earn you Planet Protector Points!

Question 1

How will you get past the mountain of rubbish?

a) Sort it into plastics, paper, metal, and food waste, and recycle it properly

b) Use your strength to shove it into a nearby river

c) Collect it all in a mountain-sized bin bag and throw it in the bin

Look at the Light

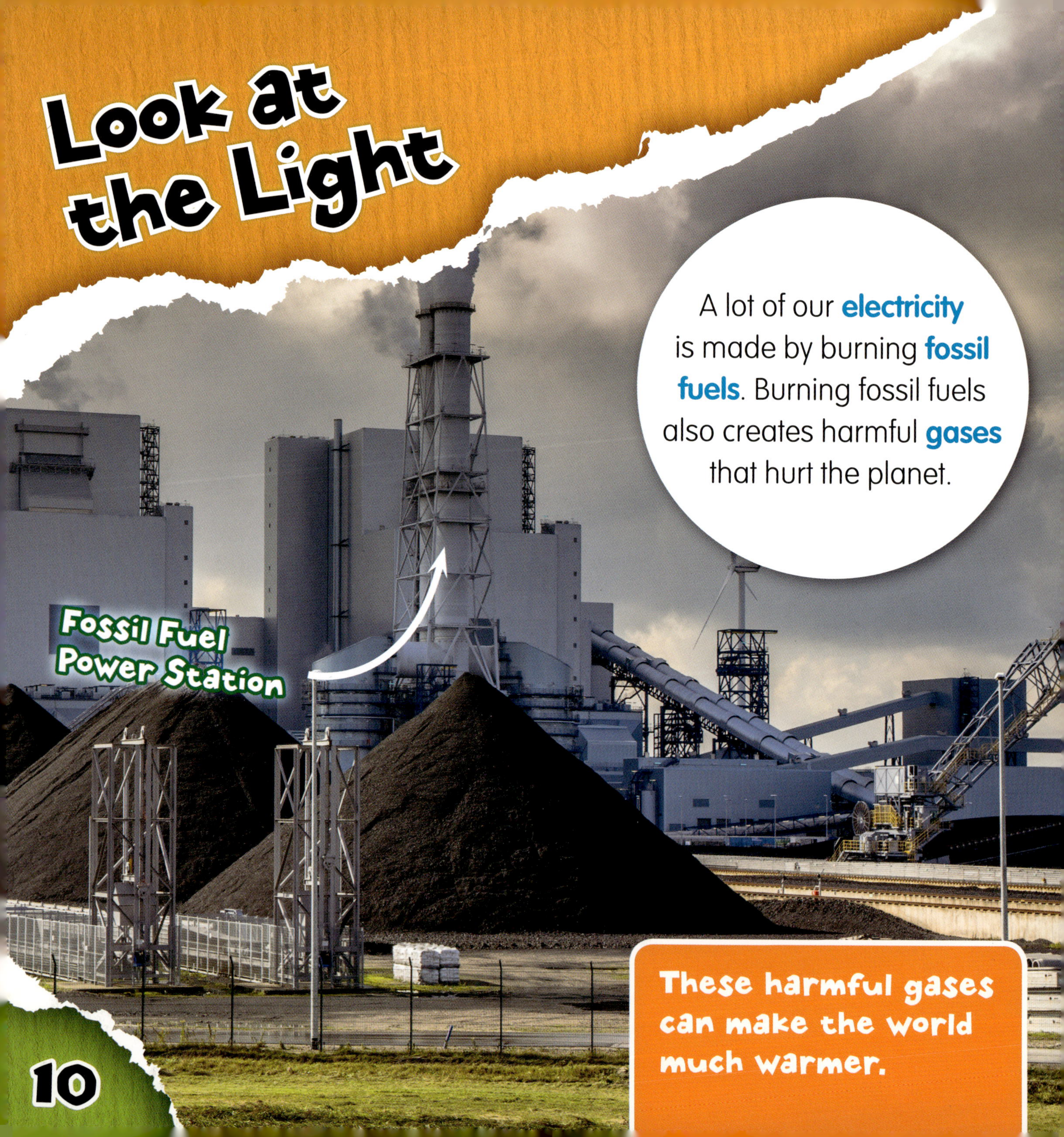

A lot of our **electricity** is made by burning **fossil fuels**. Burning fossil fuels also creates harmful **gases** that hurt the planet.

These harmful gases can make the world much warmer.

As the world warms up, many animals find it harder to survive. For example, polar bears live on **Arctic** sea ice. However, a lot of the ice is now melting away.

It is important that we all use less electricity whenever we can.

Look, it is another Planet Protector: Hydro Hero! She doesn't look happy though…

Question 2

Hydro Hero is getting angry. How are you going to light up Trashy Island?

a) Install some giant floodlights to light up the whole island

b) Throw her book away – reading is for losers

c) Get some energy-saving lightbulbs, which use less electricity

Save the Trees!

Many animals live in woodland and **rainforests** all over the world. However, lots of trees are chopped down every day for their wood. This leaves the animals without a home.

When forests are cut down, it is called deforestation.

The wood is used for all sorts of things, such as houses, furniture and even paper. These things are useful (like the paper in this book) but we should save or recycle paper when we can.

Paper can be recycled.
This is a great way to save trees.

Where have those other Planet Protectors got to? I need to send them a message about an important mission. Hmm, what is the best way to do that?

Question 3

How are you going to send a message to the Planet Protectors?

a) Send them a message using the Trashy Island supercomputer

b) Write a short note on a piece of paper, then make sure they recycle it afterwards

c) Write each one a long letter then make extra copies just in case

Farms and Food

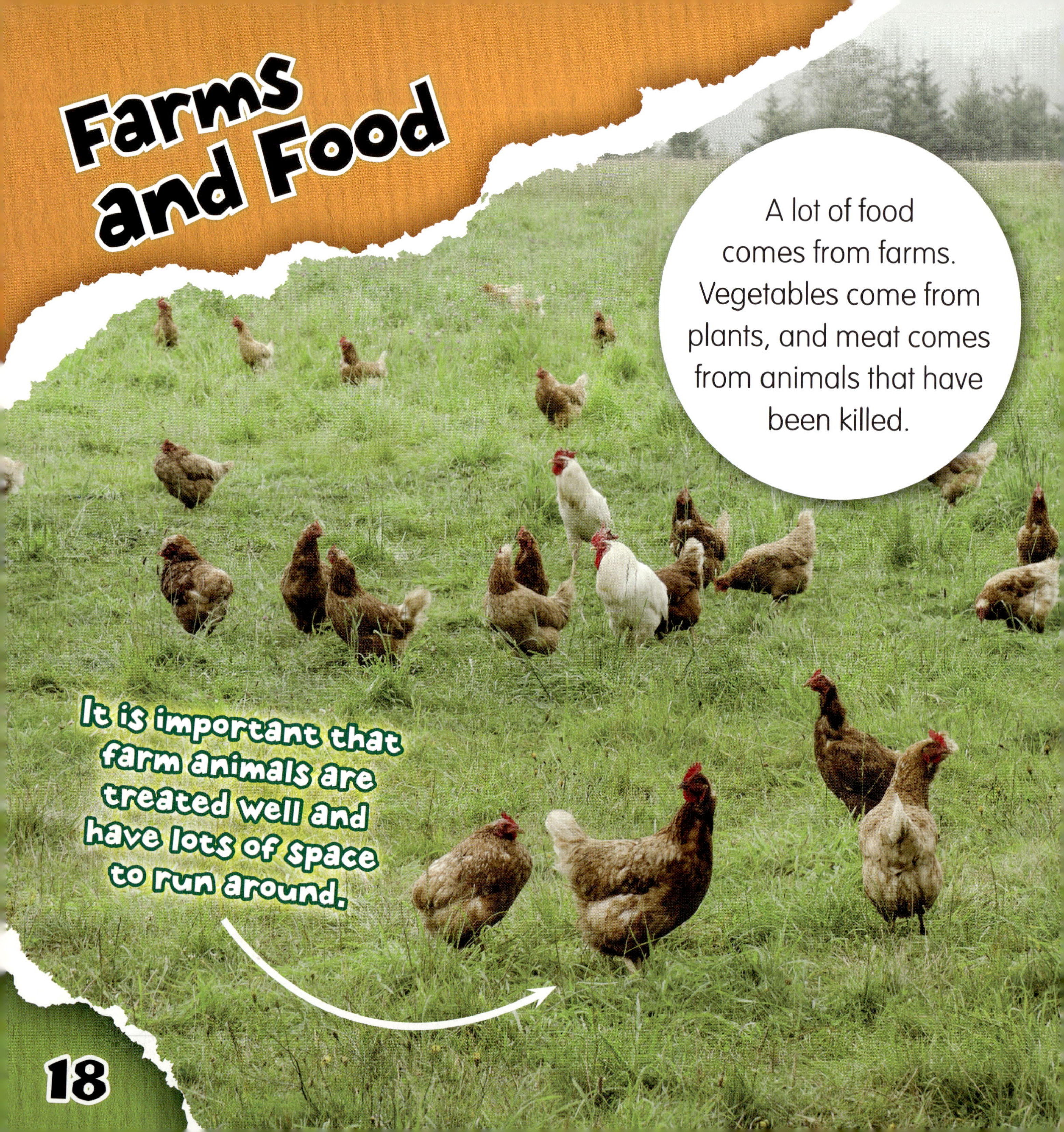

A lot of food comes from farms. Vegetables come from plants, and meat comes from animals that have been killed.

It is important that farm animals are treated well and have lots of space to run around.

Forests are cut down to make room for farmland. Lots of land is needed to keep cows. Cows also produce a gas that is harmful to the planet when they pass wind.

The more cows we keep and eat, the more dangerous it is for the planet.

Milk is also used to make cheese, yoghurt and butter.

The Planet Protectors asked me to buy some dinner, but I got stuck talking to the giraffes all day. Now I don't know what food to get for everyone.

Question 4

What are the Planet Protectors going to eat after their big mission?

a) Beef burgers for everybody

b) Cheese pizza and chips

c) Jacket potatoes and beans

A New Planet Protector?

Question 1

A = 2 points

B = 0 points

C = 1 point

Question 2

A = 1 point

B = 0 points

C = 2 points

Question 3

A = 2 points

B = 1 point

C = 0 points

Question 4

A = 0 points

B = 1 point

C = 2 points

What did you get?

0-1

Oh no! You're an environmental disaster! Try again.

2-3

You've got a long way to go before you become a true Planet Protector.

4-5

You still have more to learn. Don't worry, you'll do better next time.

6-7

Not perfect, but you did very well. You would make a good side-kick.

8

Great score! You're our new Planet Protector! You start on Monday.

Glossary

Arctic	the area around the North Pole that is made up of the Arctic Ocean and the land surrounding it
copies	things that are exactly the same
electricity	energy used to power things, such as computers and machines
environment	the natural world
fossil fuels	fuels, such as coal, oil and gas, that formed millions of years ago from the remains of animals and plants
gases	air-like substances that expand freely to fill any space available
landfill site	where waste is buried
rainforests	forests which get a lot of rainfall
recycled	used again to make something else

Index